LESSONS
FROM A
SHEEP DOG

PHILLIP KELLER

THOMAS NELSON
Since 1798

NASHVILLE DALLAS MEXICO CITY RIO DE JANEIRO

Royalties from this book are donated to Operation Eyesight International.
www.operationeyesight.ca

© 1983, 2002 by W. Phillip Keller

Published in Nashville, Tennessee, by Thomas Nelson. Thomas Nelson is a registered trademark of Thomas Nelson, Inc.

Thomas Nelson, Inc., titles may be purchased in bulk for educational, business, fund-raising, or sales promotional use. For information, please e-mail SpecialMarkets@ThomasNelson.com.

Unless otherwise indicated, all Scripture quotations are from the authorized King James Version.

Verses marked RSV are from the Revised Standard Version of the Bible, copyright, 1952 (2nd edition, 1971) by the Division of Christian Education of the National Council of the Churches of Christ in the United States of America. Used by permission. All rights reserved.

Library of Congress Cataloging in Publication Data
Keller, W. Phillip (Weldon Phillip)m 1920-
    Lessons from a sheep dog
    1. Border collies—Biography. 2. Keller, W. Phillip (Weldon Phillip), 1920- . 3. Christian life—1960- . 4. Sheep ranchers—British Columbia—Vancouver Island—Biography. 5. Christian biography—British Columbia—Vancouver Island. 6. Sheep dogs—British Columbia—Vancouver Island—Biography.
7. Dogs—British Columbia—Vancouver Island—Biography.
8. Dogs—Biography. I. Title.
    SF429.B64k44 1983   280'.4   [B] 82-16124
    ISBN 10: 0-8499-0335-1   ISBN 13: 978-0-8499-0335-9 (hard cover)
    ISBN 10: 0-8499-3130-4   ISBN 13: 978-0-8499-3130-7 (trade paper)
    ISBN 10: 0-8499-1765-4   ISBN 13: 978-0-8499-1765-3 (impact edition)

Printed in the United States of America
21 22 23 PC/LSCC 40

Contents

The Story

Lass—a Beloved
Border Collie

THIS IS A SIMPLE STORY about a special dog who shared life with me on my first sheep ranch. Though she bore the very ordinary name—Lass—she was in fact a most extraordinary dog. My memories of her companionship, loyalty, and love linger across the years as colorful recollections.

Even more important and precious, however, were the powerful, spiritual principles God enabled me to learn through working with this beautiful Border collie. Some of us are slow to grasp the basic truths of divine design. We cannot always clearly comprehend Christ's call to us in simple service. For that reason His gracious Spirit often uses the common experiences of life to shed the intense light of supernatural truth upon our path.

It is the basic principle of using parables drawn from our work-a-day world to help us clearly understand the noble, wondrous purposes of our loving Father. This Lass did for me as a young man. I was only in my late twenties when she came into my life. There were searching, burning questions in my spirit then that no sermons or studies had ever resolved in me.

Yet in His gracious, generous way God used this dog to help me see what He Himself is like in character and conduct. He taught me emphatically what His highest purposes and best intentions were for me as His friend and coworker. For He does make it very clear that as His people, He calls us to special service with Himself.

As a lad I had grown up with cattle. On our land in East Africa, my father had bred the finest of the breeds adapted to the tropics. His cattle were a special joy to him: the splendid bulls that sired our calves, the sturdy oxen that hauled our wagons and worked our fields, the handsome cows that produced our milk were a marvel to the Africans.

When I came to North America to complete my university training in animal husbandry, cattle still played an important role in my career. I worked on various ranches and longed for the day when I would purchase my own "spread" and establish my own herd.

By my midtwenties I had been made manager of one of the most beautiful ranches in the interior cattle country of British Columbia. There I was given a magnificent, courageous cattle dog named Paddy. He was excellent with our Herefords, and saved me hours of work in handling the stock.

It was shortly after this that I found a piece of neglected ranch property at the southern tip of Vancouver Island. Because it was so abused the place did not attract much interest, but I could see its potential. It was an estate sale, so cash had to be paid for the property.

The net result was I had insufficient funds left to purchase cattle, so I was obliged to start out with sheep. It quickly became obvious that dear old Paddy was completely baffled and bewildered by sheep. In disgust and dismay he began to resign himself to snoozing in the sun or sleeping by the fire.

I realized that I faced a serious dilemma with my first flock. I simply had to find a sheep dog to help me handle the ewes and lambs that grazed on my impoverished pastures. My highest hope was to come across a well-bred Border collie. For, of all the breeds, they are the finest sheep dogs.

In passing I might mention that during those initial months at Fairwinds—for that is what we called our spot by the sea—I began to wonder seriously why I had allowed myself to be stuck with sheep. Compared to cattle they seemed stupid, timid, frail, vulnerable to diseases and parasites, and easy prey to predators.

Little did I then comprehend the wondrous ways of God or His hand at work behind the scenes of my affairs. Little did I realize the enormous, eternal lessons He would teach me on those wind-blown acres where I struggled to make a beautiful county estate out of derelict land.

One day there was a short advertisement in the city newspaper. It read:

WANTED—a good country home for
pure-bred border collie.
Chases cars and bicycles.

I hurried up to a neighboring rancher's house and
phoned the owner in town, some twenty-seven
miles away. "Yes," the lady replied, "I still have the
dog. Please do come quickly. No one else wants
her." Her voice sounded desperate.

In short order I drove down the winding country road and pulled up outside a little cottage in
the suburbs. The lady was waiting for me at her
gate. Almost before I could get out of the car, she
began to talk excitedly.

"Mr. Keller, I can't do a thing with this creature. The dog is plumb crazy. She's 'loco.'" The
woman threw up her arms in dismay. "All she
does is tears after the kids, chases boys on bicycles,
jumps all the fences, and races after every car that
comes by on the road."

"Please let me see her," I requested, trying to
calm the owner's excitement. "Maybe I can do
something with her. I have had dogs all my life."

She led me around to the back of the house. As

we entered the little yard, a leaping bundle of dog flung herself toward me. She snarled and snapped, then collapsed in a heap on the ground.

Instantly, to my shock and horror, I saw the dog was not only chained from her collar to a steel post, but also was hobbled by a second chain from her neck to her back leg. What a pitiful spectacle!

Crouched in the dirt, the dog glared at me. Her ears were laid back in anger. Deep, guttural, menacing growls rumbled in her throat.

"How old is she?" I asked, my question put to the owner to help cover the profound pity and love that welled up within me. "And what is her name?"

The owner replied that the dog was two years old, and her name was Lassie.

I looked at the Border collie with mingled emotions. She was a dog gone wrong, almost beyond hope or help.

Yet somehow I saw beyond this. In her I saw a keen intelligence and a great capacity to learn. She had a splendid constitution with deep, wide chest, broad back, and strong legs. The master breeders

had done a magnificent job of producing such a superb creature.

"At two years of age, most dogs have learned all they ever will know," I remarked to the lady. "But she is too beautiful to destroy. I am prepared to give her a chance to change."

The owner was still, tense, waiting for my next words.

"I will take her home to my ranch on one condition." I weighed each word carefully. "If I cannot do a thing with her, after six weeks I will bring her back to you. She is too lovely a specimen for me to put her away. You must then destroy her."

The lady gladly agreed to my proposition. So I unhobbled Lass (from now on that would be her name). I led her out to my car and put her behind the front seat for the long ride home.

All the way I talked to her reassuringly in a gentle voice. All I got in response were low growls. Occasionally I would try to put my hand back to touch or pet her, but she would bare her teeth and snap back angrily.

Reaching the ranch, I felt a peculiar, inner assurance that somehow this torn and twisted dog would be redeemed. Our land lay at the very end of the country road where it ran into the sea. There were virtually no cars to chase, no boys on bicycles to tempt her, just the wide rolling pastures and the rugged shoreline where ocean waves thundered against the land.

Most important, there was a new master.

Lass was given a kennel with fresh, clean bedding. She had a bowl of sparkling water, and a dish heaped with food.

She would touch none of them.

Every advance made to touch her was rejected. Any attempts to call her were resisted belligerently. Day followed day. She was beginning to lose condition. And I even began to fear she might die.

In an act of faltering faith I settled on a daring step: I decided to set her totally free. The instant I did so she fled into the forest behind our cottage. In a matter of moments she had disappeared from view, and I wondered if I would ever see her again.

For several days I drove up and down the road looking for her, asking other ranchers in the area to let me know if they saw her. But there was no sign anywhere. It was as if she had simply vanished into ocean air.

Then one evening, I happened to glance up at the top of a large rock outcrop behind our home. There, on the summit, Lass lay crouched like a hunted cougar, looking down at me. I called her name, but she turned and fled.

That evening I took food and water and placed them on the rock for her. At dawn they were gone. I fed her regularly, but there was no response to any of the overtures I made to her.

A couple of weeks later a small band of sheep grazed near her lookout. I noticed she took a keen interest in them. She would cock her head, rise on her haunches, and watch them intently. Her latent instincts were coming to life.

So evening after evening, I brought up a few ewes and lambs to graze near her.

⚜

During this time, though no intimate rapport had been established between us, I felt an enormous compassion for this beautiful dog. An intense longing permeated my whole being for her to come to me, to get to know me, to trust me, to learn to love me, to work with me, to be my friend.

Yet week was following week and the time was approaching when she might have to be destroyed. It was an appalling alternative that filled me with dismay.

Then one evening the sun was setting in a golden haze over the ocean. The sheep were grazing contentedly at the water's edge. I stood entranced, my hands clasped behind my back, caught up in the wonder of it all.

Suddenly I felt a soft warm nose touch my hands. Lass had come! My heart seemed to stop with ecstasy. Contact had been made! She had found the fortitude to let me touch her life.

It was the turning point in our association.

Lass discovered that she had a new master whom she could truly trust. She had come into the care of one who really loved her, who understood her, who had only her best interests in mind.

She also began to realize that not only did I understand her, but I also knew all about sheep, ranching, and the exciting part she could play in the whole operation.

On the basis of our mutual affection and trust I began to teach her the commands so essential for success. Because of her alert mind and fine intelligence she learned very quickly. The familiar phrases and orders such as *Come—Lie down—Sit—Fetch them—Stay—To the left—To the right—* were readily understood and soon obeyed.

From voice commands, we gradually progressed to silent hand signals, so that even if she was a great distance from me she understood what to do. She would watch the movement of my right arm and outstretched hand. So she became able to handle the sheep with remarkable skill.

One of the truly touching aspects of our deepening friendship was her utter devotion to me. Where before she had been shy, distant, and antagonistic, now she became my virtual shadow. Where I went, she went. My presence was her peace and her pleasure.

She became essentially a "one-man dog." She would eat and drink only what I provided. She was mine and mine alone.

Strange as it may seem, the most difficult command for her to comply with was *Stay*. Sometimes it meant that she would have to hold a bunch of lambs in the corner of a field or guard a gate or keep watch over some unruly rams while I was doing another job. It was very trying for her to have me disappear from view. She was eager to be where the action was. She would sometimes be sorely tempted to "break faith" and take off on other tempting escapades.

Two of these were somewhat amusing, yet also posed serious problems if we were in the midst of handling the flock. The first was the colony of crows that had their rookery in the trees on a small rocky island just offshore. The black rascals would come winging in over our fields, then swoop down low over Lass to taunt and tease her.

Unable to restrain herself, she would leap to her feet and race away after her tormentors. She seemed literally to fly over the fields, her lithe and graceful body appearing almost airborne. It was a spectacular show but it did neither the sheep, the ranch, or her master one particle of good.

The second cause of her discomfiture were the great land-clearing fires we had in the winter.

Sometimes the flaming sparks and glowing cinders carried up and away in the wind were so exciting she would go leaping and bounding after them. Occasionally one would catch in her long lustrous coat and begin to burn with an acrid odor.

Lass would roll wildly in the grass, then shaking herself come racing back to me as if to say: "Well, Boss, wasn't that a grand display?" Yes it was, but it had only wasted her energies, sapped her strength, and caused her to break faith.

She could quickly sense when I was disappointed. She knew at once when a coolness came between us because of her misconduct. She would have to be corrected for her failure to be faithful in the line of duty.

These were difficult moments for both of us. But they were absolutely essential for her well-being and mine. The operation of the ranch and our success with the sheep depended in large measure upon her implicit obedience.

When the discipline was done I would gather Lass up in my arms. I would caress her head, rub her chest, and whisper in her ear, "It's all over, girl!"

Her eyes would shine again. There was total reconciliation, restoration. In pure pleasure she would leap out of my arms, race around on the grass in a wide circle, and come leaping back into my warm embrace.

Perhaps the most powerful memory that lingers with me about this delightful dog was her increasing willingness to do anything I asked of her. She was totally, instantly available for any task, no matter how tough or trying.

On the ranch we had some rather rugged, rough cut-over country. The sheep would scatter out into this difficult terrain of rock outcrops, wild rose thickets, downed timber, and windfalls. They were searching for special sweet mouthfuls of grass and leaves not grazed before.

Because of my height I always could see where the lambs and ewes were in the broken country. Lass could not. I would have to send her into these tough spots to round up and bring out the entire flock. For her it was virtually going in blind, trusting me implicitly.

"Bring them in, Lass, bring them in!" I would command her. "Don't leave a single stray behind."

She would go bounding away, over the rocks, through the windfalls, into the rose thickets. Often when she finally came out with all the flock, her face would be scratched, her fur would be clogged with burs, her feet would be cut or torn. But she had obeyed, never mind the suffering endured.

Because of such devotion and faithful service, trust and affection were built between us.

Looking back across those precious years at Fairwinds, I was learning from Lass what it was that Christ, my Great Shepherd, wanted to do with me in His fields as His coworker.

LESSON 1

❦

In the Wrong Hands

As the owner of Fairwinds, I quickly realized I would need help to run the ranch and handle the flock efficiently. That assistance had to come from a faithful, loyal Border collie, bred and disciplined for this unique work.

Though I was an energetic young man I simply could not round up the sheep alone. The flock often scattered and fled in five directions. No matter how fast I ran or how loud I shouted the sheep still strayed in their own stubborn way.

So I was obliged to find a coworker, an "undershepherd," in a sheep dog who would carry out my will in managing my flock. Working together in harmony, one good sheep dog and myself could accomplish as much as five men.

The same precise principle holds true in God's dealing with men and women. The Lord called Himself the Good Shepherd. He pictured Himself for us as the one who had come to care for the "lost sheep." He carefully instructed His disciples to be His colaborers and feed and tend His ewes and lambs.

After His resurrection, Jesus met His young friends beside the Lake of Galilee, and there prepared for them a breakfast of fish and chappatis. When the meal was over He turned to Peter, asking him three times:

"Peter, do you really love me? Are you really my friend?" When the burly young man assured the Master of his loyalty and love, Jesus responded three times by saying:

"Peter, feed my lambs."

"Peter, feed my sheep."

"Peter, feed my sheep."

This was the special labor, the unique work to which he was assigned.

It has been well said that "God has no hands in the world but our hands. He has no feet here but our feet. He has no lips but our lips." This is stating the rather obvious case that our Father God chooses to carry on His purpose through the fallible agency of common people.

He can, and does, break through into human affairs in supernatural ways. Yet in the main He chooses to use us ordinary people to accomplish His grand designs. Seen in this dimension we begin to perceive the enormous honor He bestows on those chosen to become His coworkers.

Very often, as in my first encounter with Lass, He finds us cast in the wrong role, caught in the toils of our own intransigence, abused and misused by the wrong hands of an uncaring master.

This truth struck me with tremendous impact the day I drove up to the lady's gate and heard her rant and rave about her "crazy collie." She had no inkling of how to handle such a beautiful creature, bred for special service. Nor did she seem to care that all the potential locked up in this animal had gone wrong.

It was a profound portrait of so many of us. For in the dusty dog hobbled with chains, I saw portrayed the plight of men and women who, originally destined for noble service, have fallen into the wrong hands. Now they groveled in the despair of wasted, misspent years.

The skilled master-breeders of the border counties in Britain had produced sheep dogs of acute intelligence and enormous energy. A beautiful specimen like Lass carried within her the capacity for outstanding work.

But she had to be in the right hands! She had to come into the care of a good shepherd. She had to have her old habits broken and her instincts channeled into the purposes for which she had been bred.

The same principle holds true for us. We have been created in the generous sovereignty of God to achieve great things with Him. He endows us with the capacity to carry out His will and do His work in the world, as we work together under His care. It is His intention that we should touch lives, enrich spirits, and bring souls into His care and management.

For this to happen we must be loosed from the tyranny of the wrong owner. We must be released from servitude to sin, to self, and to our slave-master, Satan.

This implies, of course, that a person is unshackled from one owner, to be brought under the management of another. There is no such thing as "absolute freedom." For even though human beings are free agents, they must come under the control of forces and influences greater than themselves.

Often, young people boast of being free to do as they wish, to go wherever they will, or become whatever they choose. This is only partially true. For though they may not realize it, their decisions, their behavior, their lifestyle are not those of their own free will. Rather, they are conditioned, shaped, and directed by the hands that govern them.

Unfortunately, Lass had fallen into the wrong hands. Under the mishandling of the wrong owner, her talent had been twisted and subverted for destructive ends. Her vitality and instincts were being wasted on chasing boys and bicycles. Her capacity for worthwhile work was expended on the empty pursuit of cars.

The upshot was, day by day, she herself unwittingly was forging the shackles of steel that bound her.

We do exactly the same. Jesus stated categorically: "Every one who commits sin is a slave to sin" (John 8:24 RSV).

Those who brag about being free seldom realize they are inexorably bound by their own destructive lifestyles. They are trapped in the toils of their own destructive decisions and desires.

Nor can they be loosed except by the loving hands of the Good Shepherd.

As I approached Lass on the day that I found her in such a forlorn state, she met me with blazing eyes, low growls, and bared teeth. She did not want me to touch her. She trembled at the tone of my unfamiliar voice.

This was not surprising. She had been misused, abused, twisted and torn in spirit. How or why should she trust anyone?

And this is precisely the same with us when first the Great Shepherd comes to us with outstretched hands. We resist His approach. We resent His voice calling us. We recoil in fear from His overtures of good will.

Doubts and misgivings surge through our minds. We cringe from His coming. Our wills are set in stern resistance. We are convinced we will suffer abuse at His hands.

But it is only the hand of God that sets us free. It is His strong hands that can train us to move in new directions. It is His gentle, yet strong, hands which can handle us with skill and love and strength. It is His hands which can change our character, alter our conduct, and send us out to do great and noble service.

The first owner Lass had did not understand dogs. She did not care about the lofty capabilities of this beautiful creature. She wanted only to get rid of Lass as quickly as possible.

Few of us think seriously about the sinister and subversive character of Satan. To many people he is almost less than real, sometimes supposed to be nothing more than a superstitious phantom or a product of man's imagination.

The terrible truth is he is very real, very active, and exceedingly deceptive. While appearing to give us liberty by allowing us to do whatever we wish in response to our own inherent selfishness or sin, he watches us enslave and destroy ourselves.

Ultimately, in the case of Lass, unless a new

owner had intervened, she would have been destroyed.

Happily that did not happen. A stranger showed up in her backyard that day. His coming would change the entire tenor of her life. This one who came saw beyond the dirt and dust that clogged her mottled coat. He saw the magnificent head, the strong constitution, the beautiful body so well proportioned. He knew the powerful potential for good locked within this tormented creature.

So bravely, boldly, I unshackled her chains and unhobbled her legs. I put my own soft collar upon her and took her to my home.

She had passed from one set of hands into another. At first it was terrifying. But one day she would know it was all very wonderful.

Many of us have been under the wrong management—in the wrong hands. We have been so mishandled that all of the original, superb purposes for which we were created have been distorted. We are virtual slaves to sin, to ourselves, and to Satan.

Yet the Stranger of Galilee comes into our lives. He looks upon us with love and sees beyond our sins. He extends His knowing hands to take us into His care.

We are not always keen to go. Life under the old master has made us suspicious. In our human ignorance we are convinced that to come into Christ's care can be even worse bondage than before.

As I put Lass into my old car and started down the road to Fairwinds she was sure something terrible was about to happen. She crouched on the floor behind my seat, trembling and tense with apprehension. It would take weeks and months for Lass to fully discover that her new master had only her best interests at heart.

It takes some of us a lifetime to learn that Christ, our Good Shepherd, knows exactly what He is doing with us. He understands us perfectly. He manages us with incredible wisdom and loving skill, both for our benefit and His.

Bless His Name!

Lesson 2

❧

Set Free—to Follow

Long before I brought Lass home to stay with us, I had painstakingly prepared a new kennel for the special dog that would share our life at Fairwinds. In my mind's eye I had pictured a Border collie that would work with me on the ranch, share in the care of the sheep, and become a virtual member of our family.

There was a new leash as well; there were also clean dishes to hold fresh food and water. Everything was in readiness for the dog chosen to be my companion and coworker. There was so much at stake in this selection. The successful operation of the ranch depended on a good dog. The skillful handling of the sheep was bound up in the creature's capacity to work obediently. My own contentment in managing the flock rested in her responsiveness to my commands.

All of these hopes, dreams, and aspirations moved through my mind as I drove home with Lass in the car. At last we pulled up at our gate. Gently I opened it, then drove to our rustic cottage perched on a rise of ground overlooking the sea.

Here in our country setting all was tranquil. Only the wind in the trees, the tide running against the rocks, the gulls and crows wheeling and crying in the breeze above the shore, broke the silence.

There would be no boys racing on bicycles. No cars roaring up the road. No traffic din or city noises to distract and disturb. Lass was coming into a new setting of quiet serenity. She was entering the life of a brand-new master. What would she do?

Her initial reaction was to slink away, crouched low in the grass, in commingled fear and foreboding. Had she not been on a long leash she would have fled into the nearby forest behind our home.

Speaking to her softly, petting her gently, I led her to the kennel standing in the shade of a lovely oak. She simply stared at it, refusing to enter. Instead she stubbornly crouched at the entrance, staring up at me with defiant eyes.

My wife, thrilled and excited by the beautiful dog, brought out a heaping bowl of food. I fetched another dish full of water for her. She ignored both of our offerings. She refused to touch either the food or drink.

This went on day after day. I was utterly dismayed. There was no sign of positive response. Her form became gaunt and wasted as day followed day.

In a bold and desperate act I undid her leash and set her free.

In a flash she was gone. Like a fleeing phantom she vanished into the woods. I wondered if ever I would see her again.

I drove up and down our country road in hope of finding her. I called at neighboring ranches. I combed our fields and ocean edge. But no sign of Lass.

In the anguish of my search, I began to understand a little of the sorrow God endures, amid all His endeavors to draw us to Him. Again and again we refuse His benefits offered to us. Belligerently we rebuff His love and concern.

Yet, in spite of her indifference and unyielding resistance, I had an enormous empathy for the dog. I longed to redeem her. I was consumed with a desire to make her into a loving, loyal companion. I yearned to see her rise to the potential that lay dormant within her.

All of these hopes seemed dashed into dust, until one evening I looked up onto the edge of a rough rock outcrop behind the cottage. There she was!

I decided to take food and water up to her lookout. Every morning it was gone. And yet every evening she would be back. Every time I approached her, called her by name, or whistled, she vanished, spirited away like smoke whisked away in the wind.

I began to wonder if this distant dog would ever become truly mine. She did not mind eating the food set out for her; she drank the water poured out for her; she relished the total freedom she had been given.

But she was not mine. Nor was I hers!

Caught up in this stand-off, the gracious Spirit

of God brought home to my heart with great clarity the predicament in which people put themselves before God.

The Master comes to us in our plight. He offers to take us into His family. He spares no pains to provide all that is necessary for our welfare and contentment. He speaks to us reassuringly. He calls us by name. He sets us totally free.

Yet the personal response of most people is to recoil from Him. They resent His approach. They refuse to respond to His overtures of compassion. They flee to escape from His hands.

The paradox in this belligerent behavior is that at the same time they do not mind taking advantage of Christ's benefits, but at the moment and place of their own choosing in their own self-willed way.

God in Christ has come and set people free. He has placed before them the benefits and delights of belonging to His family. He has made available to them His love, His care, His provisions in generous measure.

In spite of this, their liberty and freedom is used for selfish ends. They insist on doing their own thing—in their own way—at their own time. They are not under the Master's control. All the good of which they are capable comes to nothing.

One night a few ewes and lambs grazed up near the rock where Lass would lay. I saw her sit up, cock her head, and watch them with great intensity. Perhaps her latent instincts to shepherd sheep were coming to life.

Each evening when the day's chores were done, I would direct a few sheep toward her . . . hoping this might somehow help to establish contact between us.

But nothing seemed to elicit her positive response. I began to wonder if all my overtures of love were in vain. The dark prospect that she might have to be destroyed loomed ever larger.

This was the most poignant lesson I learned from Lass. It was she who eventually must make the decision whether or not she would come to me, entrust her life to my care, allow me to control her conduct.

At this point in my own walk with God I had been bewildered by the conflicting views and highly divergent doctrines debated within Christendom. Discussions on the absolute sovereignty of God as held by the extreme Calvinists, and the grave responsibility of man as taught by the Arminians had always dismayed me. For in the final analysis the issue always arises as to the ultimate end of man.

Does he decide his own destiny? Does he determine his own destruction? Does he discover that hell or heaven are of his own choice, not God's.

In my agonizing approaches and appeals to Lass I saw with intense clarity that both views were correct, complementary, and reconciled within the response of an individual's will.

As her new master, I had done everything I could within my power and sovereign love for her. Now she, in response to my compassion, would have to choose to come to me of her own free will, yet ever drawn by my overtures of concern.

The last thing in the world I wanted was to have this dog destroyed. Just the thought grieved me. I cringed from the very prospect of losing this lovely creature.

God's Word is very clear in this whole matter

He does not come to condemn us. He does not desire to destroy us.

We ourselves choose what our end shall be. We are free to follow our own feeble ways, or we are free to follow Him who came to deliver us from the despair of our own dilemma.

It was with such truths surging through my spirit that I would go out at twilight to try and draw this irascible creature to myself. Steadily my hopes grew dimmer. The crucial hour of final reckoning was just around the corner. My spirit would not always strive with Lass. Her prospects were fading.

Then one summer evening the sun was setting in a spectacle of golden glory over the western horizon. The mingled colors of rose, lavender, gold, and scarlet were reflected in the sea. In the foreground my flock fed peacefully in the pastures at the ocean edge. It was utterly breathtaking—a scene which transported one into a wondrous serenity.

But softly, almost imperceptibly amid my reverie I sensed the hesitant, first faint touch of a warm, soft nose touching my hands held behind my back.

A thrill of exquisite delight swept over me. Lass had come! The distance between us had been crossed! Irrepressible joy swept through me in wave upon wave. Hope flamed anew!

Clearly I could see now why Christ told us emphatically there was tremendous joy in heaven whenever a straying one came home. I could understand why all the hopes, desires, and dreams of God for His people, when brought to reality, set the angels singing. I could grasp why it is that in a single soul's response to God's love, there is a reason for celestial celebration.

Without being presumptuous, I felt I had stood where Christ stands, and felt as He feels, in that rapt moment when a wanderer comes to Him at last.

Lass discovered, to her delight, that what she had found was not new chains, abuse, or bondage. What she had come home to was warmth, understanding, affection, and the thrilling freedom to fulfill the purposes for which she had been bred.

All she had to do was to follow me!

It was I who would introduce her into a remarkable relationship of mutual trust, undivided loyalty, happy comradeship, and worthwhile work she had never experienced before.

As I ran my hands over her wide chest, spoke to her reassuringly in tender tones, she knew at last she was where she truly belonged.

She had found courage to put herself in the master's hands. And in this choice she had found unlimited liberty—the liberty of being a loving friend and servant.

It was a touching interlude that evening. It was a glorious moment in my life, never to be forgotten. In the fading twilight she followed me home to the cottage, quietly entered her kennel, and lay down to rest in peace and contentment.

The lesson is so clear. The choice is ours whether or not we will come to Christ our Good Shepherd.

For the person who does, it is to discover His boundless love, His enormous good will, His generous care, acceptance into His family.

In all of this there lies liberty, contentment, and total fulfillment.

Lesson 3

Learning to Trust

FOR THE FIRST FEW WEEKS of our intimate acquaintance, Lass was like a highly strung musical instrument. The lightest touch of my hands upon her made her tremble with tension. So long had she been out of tune with life that it took the new master's knowing hands a considerable time to bring her into harmony with himself. In her subconscious mind lingered the dark shadows of the abuse she had suffered in the wrong hands.

Time after time I would take her into my arms just to hold her close. At first she could endure this only for a few moments. Then with a sudden leap she would bound out of my embrace, wondering if I really meant well.

But when I brushed her thick, lustrous coat it seemed to set her apprehension at ease. When I carefully removed the burs from her body she sensed with her acute intelligence that I truly cared about her. She even learned to let me pull the angry wild rose thorns from between her toes. When the burning ceased, she would lick my hands in gratitude.

In all of these intimate contacts I began to discern that I was as much her servant as she was mine. God's gentle Spirit showed me in vivid reality the enormous condescension of Christ, who in love and self-humiliation tends my human needs.

The lesson I was beginning to learn is that God does indeed become our love-slave. He comes to comfort, to heal, to help. He comes to be our ministering companion.

In gratitude for His touch upon my life, there is born within me the desire to be His love-slave. Or to put it in the simple words of Scripture, "We love him, because he first loved us" (1 John 4:19).

This basic interchange of loving concern for each other was the bedrock upon which trust and confidence was built between this beautiful dog

and myself. Steadily she was learning what it meant to be set free into a new dimension of devotion to her owner. She was discovering the stimulus of being essential in the master's service.

Too many of us have the wrong view of work with God. We look upon it as a grim bondage or a sort of serfdom. No, no, no! For when we truly come to know His touch upon our lives, and sense the sweetness of His Spirit at work in our souls, we are liberated into joyous experiences and adventurous undertakings.

For Lass, a part of this wondrous new world of hers was the sound of my voice. She learned to listen for it. She came to understand its timbre and tone. She discovered that I meant what I said—unlike her former owner who ranted and raved, screamed and threatened in angry tirades.

When I called her she quickly discovered that she was fully expected to come. She would be petted and praised. She would be shown that her compliance and cooperation were mutually delightful.

To hear my voice was to alert herself to respond to it. For as week followed week she realized I was not one to waste words.

What I said I meant. What I told her she could trust. What I commanded she was expected to carry out.

When I spoke she would cock her ears to catch every syllable. She would tilt her head to one side, listening with intense concentration. She would fasten her eyes upon my face—alert, eager, ready to move into immediate action.

There was something very stimulating in such behavior. In this powerful response to the sound of my voice, I saw trust and confidence grow between us.

Most important, I learned from Lass how faith, likewise, grows between me and God—how acute sensitivity is established between me and my Master.

For God does speak. His voice has gone out through all the earth. He speaks through His own written Word, through His prophets of old. He speaks through Christ and through His people. He speaks through His own Spirit within us, through the wonder of His created universe.

Like Lass, do I alert myself to hear His voice? Do I set myself to be sensitive to His sounds? Do I truly concentrate on His commands? Am I ready to respond with alacrity to His wishes?

The lifetime lesson learned from working with Lass was simply this: *Faith is my personal, positive response to the Word of God, to the point where I act in quiet trust.*

This Lass was learning to do with me. This she was finding out was actually fun for both of us. It was the secret to success in our great adventures together on the ranch.

Bit by bit it was becoming clear that even when I corrected her, it was not with any ill will, but only for her good and mine. Not only was she beginning to understand that I meant what I said, but also, I said what I meant.

For me as her new master and her, as a dog in training, the excitement in seeing her twisted old traits being straightened out was a happy interlude.

Lass was moving out into a new world of fresh and exciting encounters. She had never before been set free into open fields where the wind moved over the grass in flowing motion. That same wind brought to her keen nostrils the strong stimuli of new sensations.

She was finding out all about sheep, ewes, and rams, and the frisky, gamboling lambs. She was coming across the pungent, powerful spoor of deer, raccoons, cougars, and otters. She was watching the gulls and geese and wild brant winging above the waves. She was seeing the splash and spray of the sea bursting against the rocky shore.

There was life, energy, and the pull of the natural world all around her. She was no longer a pup learning from her mother the wisdom and ways of the wild. She had to learn now from me. She had to trust me to teach her about the ranch and woods and life by the shining sea.

Amid the new surroundings of forests and fields her latent instincts were steadily being brought into harmony with the natural world around her. She was finding the role for which she had been bred, growing in the joy of living as she was intended to live, guided by my continual presence.

Lass gave me the distinct impression that we were becoming the very best of friends. She let me know that ranch life was a great game she enjoyed to the full.

But the best part for Lass, it seemed, was just being with me.

Now this is no small honor. For it places upon the one so trusted great responsibility. Her happiness was in my hands. Her contentment was in my company. Where before she had shied away from me, now by degrees she became my very shadow.

This began to make an indelible impression upon my own spirit. Searching, stabbing questions came to me as to my own walk with my Master.

Was I conscious of Christ? Did I find life with Him an adventure? Had I become so fond of His friendship that it surpassed all other interests? Was the devotion I received from this beautiful dog any measure of my loyalty to my Master?

In devastating truth I had to admit my devotion fell far short of hers. Nor would it even begin to approach her level of trust for years yet to come.

Over and beyond all this Lass became a one-man dog. She would eat only if I fed her. She would drink only the fresh water I set before her. She would permit only me to pet her intensively.

If it was necessary for me to be away, she would go on a fast until my return. She was unwilling to partake of anything offered to her by others—even my wife.

This single-minded fixation was an integral part of her personality. It was a measure of her character. Above all it was the core of our splendid success as coworkers on the ranch.

For it was based on this unwavering fidelity that I in turn could begin to trust her. I could be sure that here was a sheep dog capable of great service as we learned to work together. The future of Fairwinds and the welfare of the flock would in large measure hinge on our mutual trust and loyalty.

This is why Jesus asked Peter beside the lake, "Friend, do you really love Me? Are you really loyal? Do you trust Me?" Then, and only then could the rough-hewn fisherman be entrusted to tend the Master's flock.

And if we are serious in our desires to serve the Living Christ, we must examine carefully our relationship to Him. Can it be said of me, "He is a one-man person"? Is my devotion single-minded, centered, and concentration upon Christ? From whose hand do I eat and drink? Where do I get my nourishment and refreshment?

It was from Lass that I learned the sterling lesson that God can only truly trust those who truly trust Him. He gives Himself in wondrous plenitude to the person whose single-minded de-votion, love, and loyalty is given to the Lord.

And because of this mutual trust, those all around are enriched and blessed beyond their wildest imagination.

Lesson 4

❧

The Delight of Obedience

THE SUMMER SEASON giving way to the lovely autumn days, Lass and I were caught up in great adventures together. Handling the sheep, running the ranch, guarding against predators were more than mere work.

Rather, our life on the land was a joyous pleasure. It was from Lass that I learned the profound lesson of what it really means to please the Master—to bless God—to enrich the Spirit.

Lass was not a noisy dog. She seldom barked except to warn of a stranger's approach. When we worked together she was almost totally silent. Her energies were given to carrying out my commands. This was not always easy for she was no longer a young pup. A mature dog, already somewhat set in her ways, she had to learn to obey.

The lessons taught her were intense and un-complicated. The words of command were short and to the point: *Come, Sit, Fetch, Stay, Stop, Down, Right, Left,* and so on. They were spoken clearly, explicitly, without waste of syllables.

By degrees she learned the meaning of each. Steadily she began to respond. Every correct move was rewarded with lavish praise and hearty approval.

Strangers began to hear about this remarkable dog and would drive out from the city to watch her work with me. They would stand pensively at the gate, asking permission to see how beautifully she obeyed my commands.

The most common comments they made were, "She just loves to work with you! She enjoys car-rying out your wishes! She finds pleasure in pleas-ing you by her obedience."

In our happy hours at Fairwinds, as we went about our tasks together, there was ample time to reflect on this great lesson learned from Lass.

It became obvious to me that just as my will and wishes for this devoted dog were expressed in clear, concise terms, so likewise God's good will for me has been stated in simple, straightforward language in His Word.

God has not left us without clear instructions. His desires for us have been articulated in unmistakable terms. His Word is sharp, precise, to the point. And it is our humble responsibility to learn to respond to it.

There is among Christ's followers the element of confusion in which people claim not to understand clearly what His intentions are. There really is no excuse for this. Any person who desires to know and do God's good will can find it stated clearly in His Word.

The basic difficulty is not a lack of comprehension on our part. The question is simply the intransigence of our own unyielded wills. Most of us will not submit to the control of Christ.

The greatest delusion any man or woman can ever come under is the idea that it is a "drag" to do God's will. Just the opposite is true! Yet our old natures and selfish interests endeavor to deceive us into believing that it is a bore and bondage to serve the Master.

Part of this is associated with the traditional idea of serving God "in fear." The use of this word "fear" through the Old Testament has, most unfortunately, left the wrong impression upon our minds. And it was Lass who brought me to a clear concept of its true meaning.

To fear, with regard to God, means to reverence, to hold in such loving esteem as to be afraid of grieving the One so admired.

This was the attitude Lass held toward me. It had been built on trust and had grown gradually with the realization she could count on the consistency of my conduct and the credibility of my character. She had come to see me as more than just her master, but also her friend. We were fellow-workers in the great responsibilities of running the ranch. Her loyalty was grounded in love.

This is precisely what Jesus referred to when He spoke so intimately to His eleven disciples just before His death: "Ye are my friends, if ye do whatsoever I command you. Henceforth I call you not servants; for the servant knoweth not what his lord doeth: But I have called you friends" (John 15:14–15).

Ultimately, our love for God is demonstrated not by sentimental emotion, but rather in implicit obedience to His will, expressed in our loving co-operation with His commands.

When we comply with His wishes, our walk with Him, our work with Him, our way with Him become a deep delight. Not only is He immensely pleased, but so also are we.

It never ceased to amaze and stimulate me to see how thrilled Lass was in her whole-hearted obedience. Her eyes would sparkle with pure pleasure. Her tail would wag with joy. Her body was electric, vibrant with ecstatic satisfaction.

This is what she had been designed to do.

And precisely the same held true for me in my personal relationship with Christ. The question was, did I realize this?

Most of us do not!

I did not come into this interaction with God until I was a man well into my forties. It takes some of us "old dogs" much longer to learn new tricks than it ever took Lass to learn to love and obey me.

I confess here with burning shame that though this dear dog was a living, vibrant example of what it means to be obedient, my strong will was slow to learn this same lesson.

Lass had a lot to unlearn but she was eager and anxious to obey. At heart what she wanted was my approval.

This is a point that escapes many of us. We seem rather indifferent to whether or not our conduct meets with the Master's approval. Do we really care what He thinks of our character?

Lass, like me, had come to love Fairwinds. She reveled in all the sights and smells and sounds of the natural world pulsing around us. Each new dawn was the beginning of a bright new adventure. She was eager to learn any fresh lesson.

Of these by far the most advanced and demanding were working to hand signals, instead of spoken words of command. By combining the two together she gradually made the transition from one to the other.

For instance, if she was running toward me

at high speed, I only had to raise my arm vertically, with hand fully extended, and she would drop to the ground at once. This was the signal for *Stop!*

It was essential that she master this means of communication. First, I was often at great distances from her, almost out of voice range, so it saved shouting and yelling. Secondly, it was much less disturbing to the sheep if we communicated in comparative silence.

For this sort of command to work well between us, Lass had to learn to keep me in view and give me her constant, undivided attention.

The parallel relationship in our walk and work with our Master is most important. For as we mature in our spiritual lives we come to understand clearly the providential "hand" of God guiding us.

Early in our experiences with Christ it is imperative that we discover His will for us in and through the Word spoken. In time, this word grows so familiar, so much a force within our wills that it becomes natural for us to comply with His commands.

We then are able to sense and detect His will being expressed to us by the providential handling of our lives. We begin to look for God's hand in all the details and events of our days. We become acutely sensitive to His presence. We find our minds, spirits, and emotions concentrated on Christ, eager to do His bidding.

This does not happen overnight. Nor does it take place in one short burst of devotion. As with the long months it took Lass to learn hand commands, so it takes us years, in some cases, to sense the unmistakable hand of God directing us in every detail of our personal pilgrimage.

I know of no more exalted joy than this harmonious partnership. As I understand it, this is what it means to be a friend of God. The communion between Christ and me is very intimate and complementary. There is no strain or tension between us, but rather a superb rapport.

The end result of the remarkable collaboration between Lass and myself was the enormous benefit that came to both the sheep and the ranch because of her behavior. Through her prompt, explicit obedience the sheep were moved easily. They were handled through her swift, smooth actions with a minimum of disturbance.

Just as Lass learned to love, respect, and respond to me, so the sheep soon discovered that Lass meant them no harm, but was only carrying out commands intended for their best interests. They learned they could not outwit her, outrun her, or outflank her. Their contentment was to do what she wanted them to do, because that really was "the Master's wishes."

The ranch flourished and prospered as Lass and I were increasingly integrated into a smoothly functioning team. Everything turned on our cooperation and compatibility.

The same holds true for us in our contacts with other lives that God entrusts us to touch. If men and women are ever going to understand something of the will of God it has to be through our implicit obedience and devotion to Him. If they are to grasp the character of Christ it must be through our reflection of Him as our friend.

As I saw with Lass, this is how the Master truly intends His work to be done in this world. His work can be done with delight and it can be done so that others will benefit beneath the guidance of His great, good hand.

Lesson 5

The Test of Faithfulness

DURING OUR WORKING YEARS together, several problem areas began to appear in Lass's behavior. In a strange way, one of her greatest strengths became her greatest weakness.

It was the matter of wanting me in view at all times. Lass had a passionate fixation on being with me and in action beside me. This intense loyalty contributed enormously to her prompt obedience, and enabled her to react to my hand signals so well.

So it can be understood why the one command which she found most difficult to carry out was *Stay*. This explicit word meant for her to remain steady wherever she was placed.

On a sheep ranch, part of the success with

sheep involves moving them continuously from pasture to pasture. It also means intensive management of the flock in sorting out ewes, lambs, and rams. Only with the eager assistance of a good sheep dog can these operations be carried out efficiently and without undue disturbance for the sheep.

At such times it meant I might ask her to guard an open gate. Or she might be expected to hold a small band of ewes in a corner while I checked their lambs. Or it might be any one of a dozen other little tasks that demanded her to be steadfast, alert, and on guard while I was busy about other duties.

Lass often felt she was missing out on the action in these situations. If I disappeared from her view she was sure she had been forgotten. She would become uneasy, begin to move about, then take off in search of me.

When I came back to find her gone, it was always a severe disappointment. The sheep would quickly scatter, our work would be undone, and the task would have to be started all over again.

Lass, of course, could not fully comprehend the complexity of the work we were doing. And at times she gave me the distinct impression that for a dog as energetic as she was, to "stay" was almost asking too much of her.

God used this element in Lass to teach me a most important principle. I began to grasp the absolute necessity to be quietly steadfast and faithful wherever He placed me. In a sense these interludes in life were a test not only of my faithfulness to God, but also of His to me.

Such times of apparent inaction are not necessarily a trial for the lethargic or easygoing individual. But for the person eager to be in the thick of things, who is keen for evidence of the Master at work, these are tough and testing times. We may feel we are forgotten by God.

In retrospect, I realize that even during those years at Fairwinds I sometimes felt that way toward Christ. I often wondered why I should be stuck with this flock of sheep. I wondered why the Lord did not allow me to get into greater action in other areas of life. It was hard to see then that I was learning to be steadfast just where He put me.

At such times we do not have the greater view of the good Shepherd. We do not see His hand at work. We are sorely tempted to "break faith," to make the next move all on our own.

It has often been said that almost any of us can be heroic, even daring in the midst of great excitement. But it takes a much more steadfast faith in our Father to stay true in the quiet place where He puts us. It is in the daily duties of our little lives where God asks us to be loyal, steady friends—people who will perform their part without fanfare, those who can be trusted implicitly to do their duty.

In reflecting on those days with Lass I am still stirred by memories of times when she proved so true to me. I can recall vividly how thrilled I was to find she had stuck to her post and played her part well. How I would pat and praise her! And how she reveled in my adulation!

It is exactly the same for us. Christ will again make His presence apparent to us. He need not be grieved or disappointed. He can be given the great joy of finding us faithful in the place He puts us.

His measurement of our success does not lie in our spectacular activities. It lies in our quiet steadfastness for Him. He does not expect us to fully understand His management of our lives, but He does ask us to stay true to Him today.

❧

It was at this point in her performance that Lass was exposed to the most severe temptations. Of these by far the most tormenting was a flock of crows that nested on a nearby island.

The noisy, black rascals had chosen to establish a regular rookery in the trees that clung to the rock outcrop offshore. There in the tangle of tough branches they built their nests, laid their eggs, and reared their fledglings.

In the usual manner of these crafty birds, they were alert to any danger. They regarded Lass and me as intruders in their territory, and seemed to find some fiendish pleasure in tormenting us with their raucous cries and daring dives.

For the dog, they became a formidable temptation in distracting her from her duties. The noisy birds would come streaming out of their trees to swoop low over Lass with jeering "caws" and tormenting tactics. They would skim down just above her head, like dive bombers swooping to the attack.

The distraction was so strong that Lass would tear away after them, leaping, barking, racing over the fields in wild abandon. Her muscled frame seemed almost to float above the fields as she swept after the crows in full flight.

At times I had the clear impression that the crows engaged in this game with devilish glee. And when it was all over Lass would come back spent and exhausted, her tongue hanging out with weariness.

In one sense it all seemed very amusing. In fact she would look up into my face, her head cocked to one side, as if to say, "What great sport that was! I really put them to flight!"

Actually in another dimension it was a serious obstacle to the efficient operation of the ranch. For what the crows did was to distract the dog from her paramount duties. Their silly games wore her out and exhausted her energies for useful service. Perhaps the most disagreeable part was that the mischievous birds caused Lass to break faith and tear off after them when she was supposed to *stay*.

I often thought about the crows and how they

managed to intrude themselves into my management of the ranch. They flew in from outside the property. They were in no way a part of it. Yet their appearances every spring, when they returned from their winter migration to the south, were a signal that we had to put up with their nuisance behavior all summer.

In the contest with the belligerent birds I saw clearly a parallel that we face in our service for God. We are often distracted from the Master's highest intentions for us by extenuating events in our lives.

Circumstances which are not part of His purposes for us intrude themselves into our experience. At first appearance, they may seem harmless, even somewhat entertaining.

The difficulty is they distract us from our most important responsibilities to Christ. They call us away and tempt us to take off in hot pursuit. In the process our energies are wasted, our strength is expended—yet the benefit either to God or His flock is nil.

It may all appear as a very spectacular show. It might even seem to us a legitimate part of our service. Still, it really is not anything more than a show.

Without being unduly critical it is essential for each of us to examine our lives and ascertain what diverts us from the highest duties to which God calls us as His coworkers. Within the community of our churches it is often the temptation to entertain rather than to edify God's people. It is the desire to amuse audiences rather than instruct them in God's Word.

The temptations come in many guises. But like the crows, though they were all shining in their bright plumage, they were black rascals bent on mischief.

It seemed a fascinating irony at Fairwinds that in the autumn, about the time the crows flocked up for their fall migration, we began our land-clearing operations. With the summer work over, and the arrival of the gentle autumn rains, it was time to start tearing out underbrush and unwanted trees to provide new pastures for the flock.

Instead of crows to chase, Lass now turned her attention to the blazing sparks that would be carried into the wind from the roaring fires. As the glowing cinders drifted across the skies she would go racing and leaping after them, barking furiously.

Often in the midst of my work I would stop and watch the remarkable performance she put on. She would leap into midair snapping excitedly at the burning fragments borne aloft on the rising heat waves. Occasionally sparks would settle into her shining coat. There they would begin to smoulder, then char her hair. It gave off a repulsive stench that drifted with the cool winter winds.

In further excitement Lass would roll in the damp grass and snap furiously at the offending sparks that had set her afire. It was all very spectacular, but in reality it did not help the work on the ranch. It wore her out completely. And during those times of testing when she was expected to stay steadfast, it often took a single spark to undo all of our work.

Of course these episodes in which Lass let me down came as a keen disappointment. She sensed that she had not been faithful. Our own land-clearing fires had been her undoing.

The same principle holds true within the church, within any community of Christians, but perhaps most importantly within our own private relationship to Christ Himself.

There is the tendency to be taken up with that which is highly emotional. People are always fascinated by excitement and ecstasy in any form. The long historical record of God's dealings with His people is shot through with instances where "false fire" and "strange sacrifices" led to disaster and disillusionment. Often it has its origin within the church itself. That which was intended by God to serve His own greater purposes for good becomes a diversion to us that nullifies our usefulness.

It is worthy of consideration today that in society many of the most flamboyant "believers" often lack credibility. In their flaming zeal and inordinate preoccupation with dramatic displays there often is intermingled irresponsible sensuality that leads them astray.

There is a tendency in the church to be carried away with peripheral issues that take God's servants off on tangents. Too often the emphasis is on the dramatic rather than on the divine will of our God.

In working with Lass this lesson came home to me again and again. It is not the spectacular nor the sensational for which the Master looks. He seeks, instead, for me to simply be faithful wherever He places me in His all-wise plans and purposes.

Lesson 6

❦

Love and Discipline

It will be obvious by now that the mutual affection established between Lass and myself was very precious to both of us. It seemed to me at times that our intimate relationship was much more than merely a man and dog, more than a shepherd and his sheep dog, more even than efficient coworkers.

We had become special friends!

With her keen perception, sensitive instincts, and acute intelligence, Lass had a capacity not only to understand my commands but even to anticipate my wishes. It was this unusual awareness that made her such a remarkable worker.

Because of this harmonious cooperation between us, the livestock operation prospered and

flourished. The sheep were handled efficiently and
with a minimum of disturbance. My own work
was made much easier and more joyous. Lass herself was a totally fulfilled companion who reveled
in all her responsibilities.

I sometimes thought of our overall relationship as a triad of triumph between master, friend,
and flock—all of it possible because of the loving
co-operation of a Border Collie.

Reflecting on this happy association we enjoyed at Fairwinds, I have often thought this is
precisely the relationship Christ desires with us.
More than anything He wants me to be His companion, His coworker, His friend in helping to tend
His flock.

This is really the essence of that final discourse
He shared with His eleven disciples before His
death. It is recorded for us in great detail by John
in his Gospel, chapters 14–17. Any person who
wishes to grasp the true meaning of love for God
should read and meditate over those superb
insights.

Love for the Master is not some sentimental
emotion that sweeps over the soul in moments of

special piety. Love for Christ is a deliberate setting of the will to carry out His commands at any cost. It is the delight of accomplishing our Father's highest purposes, no matter how challenging.

The end result of such conduct is to bring sweet satisfaction to the Good Shepherd. Because of such single-minded service we sense His approval of our behavior. We know of a surety that we are loved and appreciated. And the ultimate end is that others benefit; others are blessed; others are cared for.

Jesus Himself put it this way:

> "This is my commandment. That ye love one another, as I have loved you. Greater love hath no man than this, that a man lay down his life for his friends. Ye are my friends, if ye do whatsoever I command you" (John 15:12–14).

It should be pointed out emphatically that "to lay down one's life" for another means to put the interests and wishes of others ahead of one's own. It implies that to obey Christ and carry out His intentions is more desirable than "doing my own thing."

It is one thing to put this down with pen and paper. But it is the toughest lesson any of us can learn to live out in our daily duties.

It simply is not natural for most of us to love God or love others in the dramatic discipline of a laid-down life. We are a selfish, self-serving people. We have the strange, worldly idea that to be of lowly service is to be used or abused.

Yet God in Christ came among us in lowly service. He came to minister to us, to give Himself to us. And so, because He first loved us, we in turn are to be willing and ready to love Him and others (see John 3:16–17 and 1 John 3:16–17).

As the years went by at Fairwinds, I saw in ever-increasing clarity what Jesus meant when He spoke of His love for us and our love for Him. I began to understand the true implications and demands of a laid-down life.

Continuously I was giving myself to Lass. I gave her my strength, my attention, my affection, my loyalty, my friendship, my very life.

She in turn reciprocated this outpouring by giving back to me her vitality, her vigor, her enthusiasm, her cooperation, her love, her loyalty.

Together all the benefits of this relationship were then poured out upon the flock. Our mutual energies and expertise were spent in caring for the sheep.

It would be wonderful if this sheep dog story could end here on this noble note. But it cannot. For, to be true to the tale, there were some disappointing interludes.

There were times on which Lass did break faith. There were days when she did not stay steadfast. There were many distractions that came along which drew her away from her line of duty. Love, so betrayed, demands discipline to be restored.

There were grievous interludes for her, for me, and for the flock. To correct her and to mend the breach between us there had to be discipline. This was not easy or pleasant, but it was absolutely essential.

I loved Lass far too much to let her revert back to her old, wretched lifestyle. I was too fond of her to allow her to waste her energies for naught. She was made for great things, intended for lofty service. So both of us would have to suffer to set her straight.

Discipline is never pleasant. The correction that comes with love causes pain both for the administrator and the recipient. Many of us prefer to push it all aside. We find it easier to simply brush bad behavior to one side, acting as if it did not matter.

But true love demands discipline.

If there is to be mutual trust, integrity, and loyalty again, then it must involve some suffering for us to learn this lesson.

It was not easy to punish Lass. After all, she was my friend. It demanded self-discipline on my part to insist that she perform properly, up to her full potential.

To correct her conduct with stern words or a severe reprimand or even a sharp slap made her draw back with reproach. Her bright eyes would fill with foreboding. She would lay back her ears with remorse. She would crouch low, her tail drawn down between her legs, in a hangdog posture.

For a few moments there was a distinct coolness between us. She knew full well she had failed, and she knew I was far from satisfied with her performance.

I never allowed these interludes of discipline to last long. Correction came swiftly, it came surely, yet it was over in short order.

Then I would call her to me quietly. I would speak to her softly in reassuring tones. "Lass, it's all over!" I would hold her close, rub her chest, run my hands over her head. "We're friends; all is well!"

Her eyes would begin to sparkle again as she looked up into my face. Sometimes she would reach out to lick my cheek with her tongue. Her body would quiver and she would begin to move her tail with pleasure.

The strict discipline had brought total restoration of trust between us. We were fond and loyal friends again. Her highest good had been served. The best interests of all of us had been preserved.

For me the entire area of God's discipline of my personal life was best learned from Lass. Through such examples I came to understand implicitly what my Master's intentions are for me during those times when He corrects my conduct.

As the Spirit of God makes abundantly clear in Hebrews 12:6-11, "For whom the Lord loveth He

chasteneth . . . (disciplines) . . . . Now no chasten-
ing for the present seemeth to be joyous, but grievous: nevertheless afterward it yieldeth the peaceable
fruit of righteousness unto them which are exer-
cised thereby."

For years there has been prominent in the
church an unbalanced overemphasis upon the
love of God. There has been a universal tendency
to teach that Christ is so compassionate, so kind
that He does not discipline us for wrongdoing.
There is the false impression that any old thing
can go on, that God will simply forgive and for-
get all about it.

This simply is not so. There is a price to pay for
our perverseness. There is a discipline we deserve
for wrongdoing. There is the Master's demand that
we be faithful in service, serious in our responsibilities to Him and others.

We distort the true character of Christ if we
assert that He will merely wink at wrong. He is
grieved when we deliberately disobey His commands and selfishly ignore His wishes.

When Peter betrayed his Master the night
before His crucifixion, it took one searching look

to shatter the man's soul. He went out into darkness to break down in tears and remorse. In burning shame he was reduced from a tough, cursing fellow to a soul-shattered penitent.

Yet this was the man so swiftly restored after the Master's resurrection. He was the servant spoken to with such reassurance beside the lake, "Peter—do you love Me?—Then feed My sheep!" Three times over in a triad of tenderness the bonds of trust, love, and loyalty were reestablished between Jesus and His friend.

Like Lass we shrink back from the discipline of God. We find it grievous. We would rather it was set aside.

It cannot be. It is for our best. It is for His benefit. It is for the eventual blessing of others whose lives we touch.

And when it is all over, the bonds of affection between Christ and ourselves are even stronger than before. For instinctively, deep within our own spirits we know we deserve discipline. We know the Master would not be true to Himself or to us if He simply let our misconduct slide into sinister selfishness.

He disciplines because He cares, because He loves, because He heals.

With this reassurance comes renewed joy. There is total restoration. There is sheer delight in once again doing His bidding.

Lesson 7

❧

Available for Anything

PERHAPS THE MOST UNFORGETTABLE lesson I learned from Lass can best be summed up in three words: *Available for Anything*. The realization that though she was only a dog, she exhibited this remarkable trait in all of our years together, was tremendously challenging.

In this story I have tried to convey some of the love, loyalty, and excitement we shared as master and friend. Yet of all these varied experiences it was ultimately Lass who taught me best what it really means to be utterly abandoned to the Master's purposes. She showed me in her loving devotion what it costs to be always available for anything that needed to be done in the interests of the ranch and flock.

This principle is best understood by recounting two entirely different types of duty she was expected to carry out.

The first had to do with gathering up or counting sheep. Because of the very character of sheep—their helplessness, susceptibility to disease, and vulnerability to predators—they must be ever under the owner's constant scrutiny.

By far the surest way to make certain all is well is for the sheepman to take a count every day. In this way he knows at once if every sheep is free from harm.

I can recall the sense of foreboding that would sweep over me whenever I went into the pasture and found that one or several of the ewes or lambs was missing.

I can still sense the despair that flooded over me when I came out in the morning to discover that either a cougar or stray dogs had wrought havoc among the flock during the night. Dead sheep or torn lambs would lie strewn in the fields. And only an accurate count would determine the devastating losses.

On other occasions, when the flock were fat

and flourishing on the fallen acorns, it was quite common for the choicest ewes to become "cast"— unable to get back on their feet. They would soon die unless I found them in time to turn them over.

It was always an ominous sign when the dark-winged buzzards wheeled in the sky above our terrain. Immediately I knew they were watching for a hapless sheep that might soon provide them with a gory banquet at its carcass.

I would call Lass. "Well, girl, we'll have to gather up the sheep today!" She would race to my side, eager to go anywhere, anytime.

Some of our land lay in beautiful open fields with occasional clumps of trees scattered over it like a lovely English park. Other parts were wild and rough, especially along the shoreline. Some of this was rocky, with great granite outcroppings. Amid the boulders there were patches of wild roses, thorny blackberry tangles, old stumps, and down timber.

The sheep loved to work their way into these spots searching for stray patches of sweet grass or other dainty herbs they relished. It was no easy thing to find all the flock is such difficult cut-over country. But this was an important part of the work entrusted to Lass. I would send her to fetch out every straggling, stray ewe and lamb.

"Fetch them in, Lass!" I would command her. "Go out and bring them home!" Without hesitating an instant she would be gone, pushing through the undergrowth, running over the rough rocks.

It was stimulating to watch her work with such enthusiasm. She flung herself into the task until every sheep was brought out.

There was a cost to the dog in all of this. She would become very weary. Her face would be scratched and torn by the thickets. Her coat would be clogged with burs and debris. Sometimes the pads of her feet would be lacerated with the sharp stones.

Yet she went gladly, with happy abandon. She knew I knew what I was doing. And all she desired was to be a dynamic part of the whole project. Not once did she hesitate to hurl herself into the toughest tangle to gather up the flock.

Her selfless abandonment to my wishes made an enormous impact upon me. in quiet moments of reverie I would ask myself the soul-searching questions: "Am I this available to my Master? Am I as willing to fling myself into His work? Am I so devoted to Him? Does the matter of suffering deter me from duty?"

More often than not Lass put me to shame.

Reflecting upon all of this I began to see why it is that Christ calls us, as His coworkers, to go into tough places. Being His friend is no cozy guarantee that life will always be either easy or even agreeable. There are simply bound to be some tough assignments, some suffering if we are to fully comply with His commands.

I never sent Lass into hard places to hurt her. But I put her into challenging circumstances to save the sheep. And it was out of all these endeavors together that she gradually matured and developed into a magnificent worker.

All of us as God's people seem to shrink back from suffering. We are so often reluctant to undertake even the smallest assignment for the Master. We are reluctant to share our strength, time, or talents to touch others in trouble. We draw back from the distasteful situation where we might have to suffer a bit in order that others might be saved.

I saw all of this vividly as I worked with Lass. Her shining spirit and eager abandonment to my wishes combined to form a highly polished mirror in which I clearly saw reflected all the flaws of my own character—the failings of my own conduct toward Christ.

God's gracious Spirit used the hearty service of that beautiful collie to break some of my own tough resistance to His will for me. If she could be so instantly available for anything, surely I could do as well for God.

Many of us fail to realize what a noble honor it is to be called the friend of God. We are not often shown what a stirring challenge it is to be called to suffer with Him. We do not seem to see that amid all the varied vicissitudes of life He really does know what He is doing with us. He can grasp the whole scheme of things and see far beyond our finite view. He is utterly in command and control of every situation.

Then let us trust Him fully. Let us follow Him fearlessly. Let us fling ourselves with glad abandon into His enterprises.

This Lass did with me—even in the darkest

night and most dangerous engagements. This was the second way in which she proved her loyalty.

As the years went by at Fairwinds our happy times together were interspersed with challenging events that demanded extra determination for us to survive.

The most frequent were attacks from both cougars and stray dogs at night. We lived close to wild country where there were forested hills and wilderness terrain. From time to time the cunning panthers would come out of the dense forest and raid the flock.

To warn us of the predators' stealthy approach at night I put bells on the sheep. If the sheep were startled in the dark they would leap to their feet and flee for their lives. The wild tinkle of the bells awakened me from sleep.

I would leap out of bed, grab my flashlight, take the well-worn .303 rifle that stood by the door, and dash out into the fields. One never knew whether the sheep were being molested by stray dogs, cougars, or rustlers.

For where we lived, most of the ranchers kept sheep, and rustling had become quite common in

our part of the country. Men in trucks would back up to a fence, cut the wire to make a wide opening, then send their trained dogs into the pastures to round up a bunch of sheep, driving them right into the truck to be hauled away.

As I left the house in the dark, Lass would instantly be at my side—no need to even call her. With experience she, too, had learned to listen for the alarmed jangle of sheep bells ringing when the flock fled.

Leaping joyously beside me she would bound up in the dark and lick my hand as if to say, "Cheer up, Boss. This is a great adventure!" So off we would go side by side to see what the danger was.

It always surprised me how quickly the sheep sensed that we had come to protect them. They would soon start to relax and graze quietly again or even lie down peacefully in the pastures.

Yet in all of this there was real danger for both Lass and myself. Rustlers were not averse to shooting the rancher's dog. Nor were marauding dogs slow to attack another strange dog in the dark. Even the presence of a panther on the prowl was enough to make us doubly alert to any danger.

But Lass seemed to revel in this excitement. Not once did I ever see her cringe from our night forays in fear. Never did she decide she would rather remain in the cozy comfort of her kennel.

Some nights she and I would actually spend the entire night keeping watch in the fields. I would rest quietly in the grass, the rifle over my knees.

She would lie crouched on guard beside me. Her head often rested on my lap, but her eyes never closed; her ears were ever alert for the faintest strange sound. If anything aroused her a deep growl would rumble in her chest and I would be ready with the rifle.

These were intimate interludes for both of us. We were in this thing together. It was the tough way to meet a tough challenge, but we simply had to be on guard. Because of it we were able to keep the sheep from danger and protect them from their predators.

The Lord used Lass to teach me still another truth about Himself in the dark and difficult episodes in life! He is always there! He is fully alert and aware of the dangers abroad! He spares Himself no pains to protect us from those who would imperil our lives!

It is well to remind ourselves often of the utter faithfulness of God. We are too prone to believe that He really is not with us, that He does not know what dangers confront us, that He is out of touch with things!

Lass helped me to understand that it is often in the darkest hour, during pressing danger, that the Master is closest to us. He cares, and He cares profoundly. It is His presence which gives us peace. It is His nearness which gives us hope. It is His protection which gives us life.

Amid this He enjoys our company. He loves to have us alongside. He, too, finds consolation in the eager, alert watchfulness of His friends. In the midst of our danger there is delight. We need not be alarmed or anxious.

He is here!

All is well between us! Bless His wondrous name!

About the Author

W. PHILLIP KELLER (1920-2001) was born in East Africa and trained as an agronomist. He worked as an agricultural development specialist, wildlife photographer, and naturalist, and further expressed his love for nature and its God in many bestsellers, including *A Gardener Looks at the Fruits of the Spirit, Wonder O' the Wind*, and *A Shepherd Looks at Psalm 23*. Keller was a graduate of the University of Toronto and Brooks Institute of Photography in California. A popular author and lecturer, Keller's writing was inspired by in-depth Bible study, intense prayerful meditation, and his passion for sharing spiritual truths with people of various nationalities.